POP CULTURE BIOS
SUPERSTARS

CODY SIMPSON

POP STAR FROM DOWN UNDER

HEATHER E. SCHWARTZ

Lerner Publications Company
MINNEAPOLIS

To my beautiful nieces,
Maya and Hannah Bloom
and Sarah Axtell

Copyright © 2014 by Lerner Publishing Group, Inc.

All rights reserved. International copyright secured. No part of this book may be reproduced, stored in a retrieval system, or transmitted in any form or by any means—electronic, mechanical, photocopying, recording, or otherwise—without the prior written permission of Lerner Publishing Group, Inc., except for the inclusion of brief quotations in an acknowledged review.

Lerner Publications Company
A division of Lerner Publishing Group, Inc.
241 First Avenue North
Minneapolis, MN 55401 U.S.A.

Website address: www.lernerbooks.com

Library of Congress Cataloging-in-Publication Data

Schwartz, Heather E.
   Cody Simpson : pop star from down under / by Heather E. Schwartz
     p.   cm. — (Pop culture bios: Superstars)
   Includes index.
   ISBN 978–1–4677–1305–4 (lib. bdg. : alk. paper)
   ISBN 978–1–4677–1769–4 (eBook)
   1. Simpson, Cody, 1997– —Juvenile literature. 2. Singers—Australia—Biography—Juvenile literature. I. Title.
ML3930.S569S38 2014
782.42164092—dc23 [B]   2013001164

Manufactured in the United States of America
1 – BP – 7/15/13

INTRODUCTION PAGE **4**

CHAPTER ONE
AWESOME AUSSIE
PAGE **8**

CHAPTER TWO
AMERICA'S NEXT BIG STAR
PAGE **14**

CHAPTER THREE
LIVING THE DREAM
PAGE **20**

CODY PICS!	28
SOURCE NOTES	30
MORE CODY INFO	30
INDEX	31

INTRODUCTION

Cody Simpson performs in New York City in October 2012.

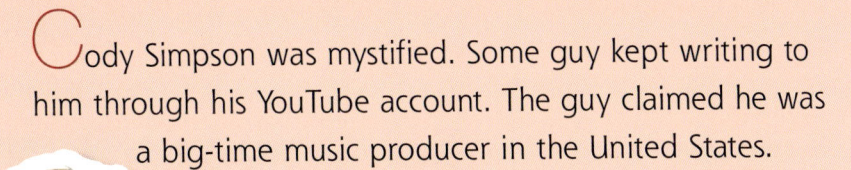

Cody Simpson was mystified. Some guy kept writing to him through his YouTube account. The guy claimed he was a big-time music producer in the United States. Not only that, but he'd seen Cody's videos and thought the young crooner was talented. He wanted to work with Cody.

Hmmm…Cody loved playing guitar and singing on the videos he uploaded to YouTube. But this sounded way too good to be true. The messages kept coming, though. And they were getting harder to ignore.

Cody was twelve years old. He knew he needed help dealing with this situation, so he shared the messages with his parents. Their reaction?

MUSIC PRODUCER = a person who supervises the work of musical performers and helps them create the best music they can

Skeptical. Suspicious. And who could blame them? But they were also willing to consider a happier ending to the developing drama. So together, the Simpson clan Googled the guy to get the straight scoop. They typed in his name: Shawn Campbell.

They couldn't believe what they found out. Shawn Campbell was telling the truth! He *was* a music producer. He was tight with some of the biggest names in the industry: Jay-Z, Foxy Brown, Missy Elliott. It was time to set up a time to talk with him.

The Simpsons agreed to chat with Shawn by Skype. Cody played some of his original songs during the call.

Cody poses for a photo with music producer Shawn Campbell (LEFT) and actress Jessica Szohr in August 2010.

By the end, Shawn wanted to book a recording session with Cody at Shawn's studio. If all went well, Shawn could help Cody develop a career in music.

Saying yes meant a 'round-the-world trip for Cody. He and his dad left their home in Queensland, Australia, for the studio in the United States—in Frederick, Maryland, to be exact. From their first recording session, Shawn was impressed.

"I didn't have any intentions to become a singer professionally. I love to sing and stuff, but it just hadn't really crossed my mind," Cody dished in an interview years later. **"I'm grateful that it's happened and it's just real fun. I love it."**

Cody performs in Los Angeles in October 2012.

Cody with his mom, Angie

CHAPTER ONE
AWESOME AUSSIE

Cody hangs out backstage with his dad, Brad, in December 2011.

These days, Cody's famous for his lyrics about love and life. But his first song? It was about putting diapers on chickens. Even he doesn't remember what *that* was about. **"Who knows what my seven-year-old brain was thinking?"** he says now.

Cody was just a tiny tyke when he penned his first original tune. But he had plenty of inspiration. He liked country music by Keith Urban and Johnny Cash. Cody's own dad was another fav performer. Cody grew up listening to his dad sing and play guitar for friends at parties. He asked his parents if he could take lessons. A few sessions later, his guitar teacher called home. Trouble? Not a chance. She was blown away by Cody's talent!

Singer…or Swimmer?

Growing up, Cody kept playing and writing more songs. But he didn't have any big plans to be a musician. That kind of life was in the United States. To an Aussie, it seemed so far away. Besides, he wasn't *just* a musician. He was also a competitive swimmer—and a good one at that. His coach hoped he'd aim for a spot on the 2016 Olympic team. Even Cody thought he'd like to be the next Michael Phelps.

By the age of ten, Cody hadn't quite nailed down his future plans. He knew one thing for sure, though. He wanted to be famous for something. With that in mind, he talked to his mom about buying the domain name CodySimpson.com. It took some convincing, but she finally agreed.

Cody once dreamed of being an Olympic swimmer like Michael Phelps (LEFT).

YouTube Talent

When Cody was eleven, he performed in public for the first time. The venue: a school talent show. The song: "I'm Yours," by Jason Mraz. He sang a duet with his sister's friend. Afterward, the friend wanted to post their performance on YouTube. That sounded like fun to Cody, so he created an account. Then he started uploading more videos—of solo performances.

Some of the videos featured Cody's original songs. Others were covers of songs written by musicians he admired, such as Justin Timberlake, the Script, and the Jacksons. He was psyched to get a few hundred views.

In less than a year, his videos caught Shawn Campbell's attention. Cody's hobby was about to become a real job.

Jason Mraz scored an international hit with his song "I'm Yours" in 2008.

COVERS = new versions of existing songs

Cheerio, Australia, and G'day, L.A.!

Cody was a sixth grader when he was discovered. When word got out, some of the other kids at school teased him. They said that singing was stupid—and that pursuing a career in music was even more uncool. They wouldn't stop laughing at Cody.

But Cody didn't have time for haters. After meeting with Shawn in September 2009, he made a trip back to record his debut song as a pro singer. Called "iYiYi," it was a catchy tune about missing a girl he liked (maybe a crush back in Australia?). He also signed a deal with Atlantic Records.

BUH-BYE, BULLIES!

When Cody made it big, he used his superstar status to help support Defeat the Label, a national campaign against bullying.

DEBUT = first. A debut song is the first song recorded by a musical act.

By June 2010, the Simpsons had left their home to stay with Cody's aunt. It was the final step before they left Australia. Cody's team was ready to introduce him as the world's next big pop star. The whole family was moving to Los Angeles so Cody could get started.

Cody with his brother, Tom (CENTER), and sister, Alli, at an event in May 2012.

BITE-SIZED CODY BIO

Birthdate: January 11, 1997
Middle name: Robert
Nicknames: Cod-fish, Codes
Parents' names: Angie and Brad Simpson
Siblings: Tom and Alli (both younger than Cody)
Height: 5 feet 11 inches (1.8 meters)

Cody hangs out on the balcony of his family's Los Angeles home in 2011.

CHAPTER TWO

AMERICA'S NEXT BIG STAR

Cody performs in Miami, Florida, in December 2010.

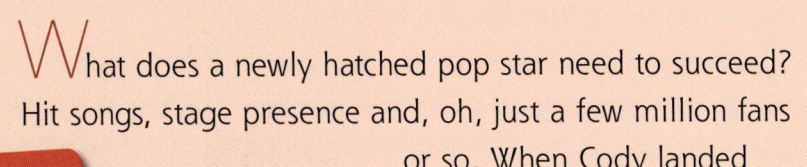

What does a newly hatched pop star need to succeed? Hit songs, stage presence and, oh, just a few million fans or so. When Cody landed in the United States, he had plenty of work to do. His first big assignment: a nationwide tour with other young musicians. Cody was stoked. It was a lifelong dream come true!

On the Camplified 2010 tour, Cody crooned at summer camps all around the country. This was his chance to practice playing in front of live audiences. He definitely had to get used to the screaming fans. They just couldn't help themselves when the blond cutie stepped onstage.

SWAK

During the Camplified tour, Cody started signing his autograph with Xs and Os. Swoon!

Cody on tour at Six Flags theme park in Austell, Georgia, on August 4, 2010

Later that year, Cody released his debut EP, *4U*. The EP featured two versions of "iYiYi" plus three new songs. One of them, "All Day," became a No. 1 hit on Radio Disney. Now he had even more tunes to offer fans.

EP = a recording that is shorter than a standard album. EP stands for extended play.

Tour, Tour, and Tour Some More

In spring 2011, Cody hit the road on his second U.S. tour. This time, he was a co-headliner with singer Greyson Chance. Cody and Greyson hit it off right away. Both were skateboarders. They loved playing PlayStation on the tour bus they shared. And they did their schoolwork together too.

Greyson Chance (LEFT) and Cody toured together in 2011. Like Cody, Greyson found success after posting videos on YouTube.

HEADLINER = the main performer on a tour

Cody (RIGHT) and Greyson (LEFT) during the Waiting 4U tour in May 2011.

When that tour ended...Cody went on tour *again!* This time, he traveled back to Australia. He might have expected a warm welcome from his homeland fans. And for the most part, he got it. But when he played in Sydney, someone threw eggs at him. Cody didn't want to disappoint the thousands who'd come to support him. He kept the show going and stopped only when security shut things down.

INSIDE CODY'S TOUR BUS

The bus Cody shared with Greyson Chance was stocked with cereal and Mountain Dew. Cody couldn't live without either one!

ROOM FOR IMPROVEMENT

Sure, he's got natural talent. But Cody's not on an ego trip about it. After arriving in the United States, he worried about his lack of real training. He honed his skills with singing and dance lessons.

Practice Makes Pro Performer

After Australia, Cody returned to the United States for his Coast to Coast tour. This time, he visited malls across the country. Each performance drew thousands of screaming fans. By then, he knew how to deal. He wore an ear monitor during shows to block out the sounds of the crowd.

Cody gives an outdoor performance in Indianapolis during his Coast to Coast tour in 2011.

When Cody released his second EP—*Coast to Coast*—in September 2011, it ranked No. 12 on the SoundScan/*Billboard* 200 chart. A song from the EP, "On My Mind," reached No. 1 on Radio Disney. And Cody's "On My Mind" video got more than 14 million views on YouTube.

By the end of 2011, Cody had worked his butt off—and it showed. He had hit songs and millions of true-blue fans. He was a genuine pop star.

CHAPTER THREE
LIVING THE DREAM

Cody was totally devoted to his career. When asked about his love life, he even told reporters he was too busy for romance. He was dating his music! He had to take a break sometimes, though. When he wasn't touring, recording, visiting talk shows, getting through school with a tutor, and winning awards—whew!—he liked to surf, play golf, and chill with his Australian mates.

CODY + KYLIE = <3?

Reporters had a field day when they spotted Cody hanging out with Kylie Jenner, the star best known for appearing alongside her family on the reality show *Keeping Up with the Kardashians*. Rumors flew that the two may be a couple. Cody and Kylie do love spending time together. However, both celebs insist they're just good friends.

Cody and Kylie caused a buzz when they were spotted together at The Grove shopping center in Los Angeles in November 2011.

Cody on the Welcome to Paradise tour in February 2012.

In 2012, Cody turned fifteen. But there wasn't much time for normal teen activities. In February, he headlined his own Welcome to Paradise tour across America.

In March, he attended the 2012 Nickelodeon Kids' Choice Awards (wearing all white, with sister, Alli, by his side) and won the first ever Favorite Aussie Superstar award. That summer, his interactive movie, *Finding Cody*, premiered on The Warner Sound YouTube channel. He also toured as an opener for Big Time Rush.

Cody brought his sister, Alli, to the 2012 Nickelodean Kids' Choice Awards.

In September, Cody spent a week performing as an opener for Justin Bieber. He also released his first full-length album, *Paradise*. The album featured ten songs, and Cody helped write most of them, taking inspiration from favorite artists such as Jason Mraz, John Mayer, and Jack Johnson.

> OPENER =
> a musician who is the first to perform

SIMPSON VS. BIEBER

When Cody first hit the scene, a lot of people started calling him the next Justin Bieber (RIGHT). And the singers *do* share a lot in common. Lots of girls crush on both the stars. Both guys sing fun, upbeat pop songs. And both were discovered on YouTube. Cody told *PopStar!* magazine he was flattered by the comparison.

Sensitive Soul

When asked about the "paradise" theme, Cody had a heartfelt answer. He visited Australia only once or twice each year these days. Paradise meant home for him—a place far from the ups and downs of being a star.

Cody's paradise is Australia. He grew up in Gold Coast, Queensland.

GIVING BACK

Cody's packed schedule has always included charity work. In 2012, he showed his support for PETA (People for the Ethical Treatment of Animals) by appearing in an ad with his dog, Buddy.

WHAT'S A SIMPSONIZER?

Cody's fans are called Angels and Simpsonizers.

Cody loved stardom, but it was strange seeing girls scream and cry at his shows. And why was everyone so interested in his love life? He sometimes dreamed of getting away from it all.

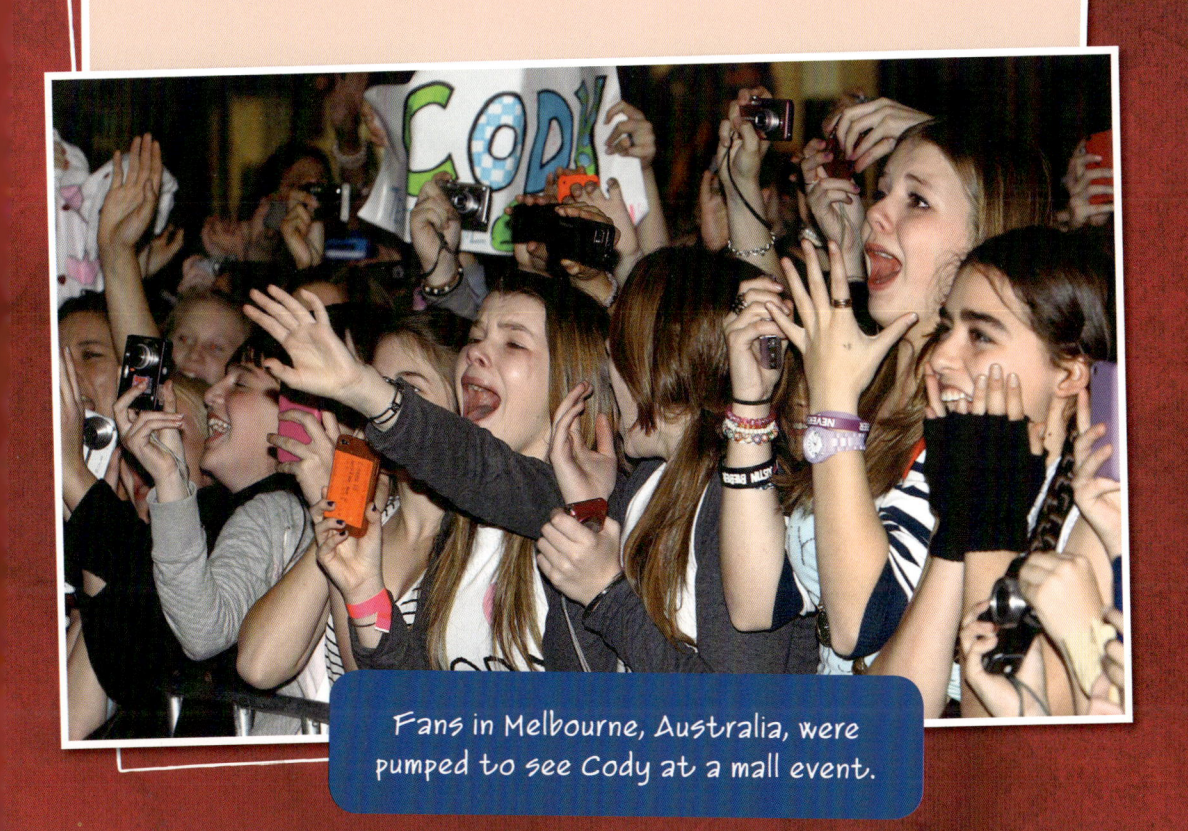

Fans in Melbourne, Australia, were pumped to see Cody at a mall event.

Cody rocks the stage in March 2013.

Yet, for the most part, Cody took his new life in stride. The love from his fans was pretty easy to get used to! By 2012, his YouTube views numbered more than 120 million. He had more than three million "likes" on Facebook and more than three million Twitter followers. Not too shabby!

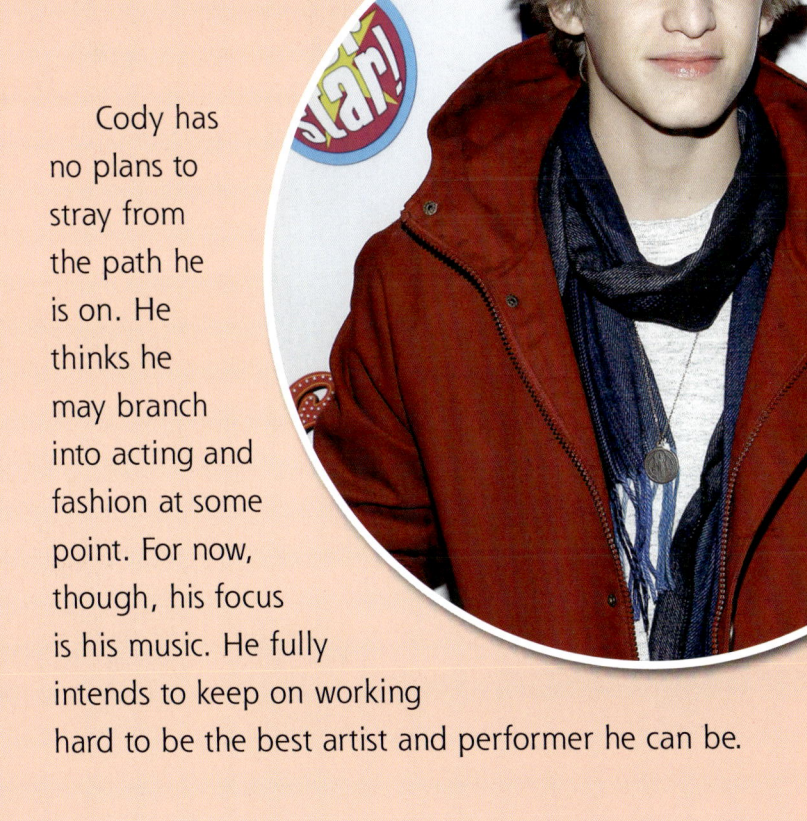

Cody has no plans to stray from the path he is on. He thinks he may branch into acting and fashion at some point. For now, though, his focus is his music. He fully intends to keep on working hard to be the best artist and performer he can be.

CODY PICS!

Cody and Carly Rae Jepsen (RIGHT) were both opening acts on Justin Bieber's Believe tour in 2013.

Cody onstage in Glasgow, Scotland, on February 19, 2013

SOURCE NOTES

7   Ratha McCann and Marie Morreale, "Ink Splot 26: Cody Simpson," *Scholastic Inc.,* January 20, 2012, http://blog.scholastic.com/ink_splot_26/2012/01/cody-simpson.html (January 13, 2013).

9   Melanie Herr, "Teen Star Cody Simpson Came By His Love of Performing Early," *Lancaster Online*, August 9, 2012, http://lancasteronline.com/article/local/709907_Teen-star-Cody-Simpson-came-by-his-love-of-performing-early.html (January 13, 2013).

MORE CODY INFO

Cody Simpson Music
http://www.youtube.com/user/CodySimpsonMusic
See Cody where it all started—on his YouTube channel.

Cody Simpson Official Website
http://www.codysimpson.com
Check out Cody's official website for upcoming shows, music, and more.

Cody Simpson on Facebook
https://www.facebook.com/codysimpsonmusic
See Cody's latest pics and bond with other Angels and Simpsonizers.

Cody Simpson on Twitter
https://twitter.com/CodySimpson
Follow Cody for updates while he's on the road.

Higgins, Nadia. *Justin Bieber: Pop and R & B Idol.* Minneapolis: Lerner Publications, 2013.
Lots of people say Cody and Justin are similar. Read this bio all about the Biebs and see what you think!

Troy, Michael. *Fame: Cody Simpson.* Beverly Hills, CA: Bluewater Productions, 2013.
Learn more about Cody's journey from regular kid to celebrity sensation in this comic book biography.

INDEX

"All Day", 16
Atlantic Records, 12

Bieber, Justin, 23

Campbell, Shawn, 6–7, 11–12
Camplified, 15
Chance, Greyson, 16–17
Coast to Coast (EP), 19
Coast to Coast (tour), 18

Finding Cody, 22
4U, 16

"iYiYi", 12, 16

Jenner, Kylie, 21

Los Angeles, 13

"On My Mind", 19

Paradise, 23–24
PETA, 24

Queensland, 7

Simpson, Alli, 13, 22
Simpson, Angie, 5–6, 9–10, 13
Simpson, Brad, 5–7, 9, 13
Simpson, Tom, 13

Welcome to Paradise, 22

YouTube, 5, 11, 19, 22–23, 26

PHOTO ACKNOWLEDGMENTS

The images in this book are used with the permission of: © Joe Kohen/Getty Images, pp. 2, 27; © Larry Marano/Getty Images, pp. 3 (top), 8 (left), 20 (bottom left); © Mark Metcalfe/Getty Images, pp. 3 (bottom), 20 (top); © Kevan Brooks/AdMedia/ImageCollect, p. 4 (top left); © Moses Robinson/Getty Images, p. 4 (top right); © Astrid Stawiarz/Getty Images, p. 4 (bottom); © Jamie McCarthy/Getty Images, p. 5; © Christopher Polk/WireImage/Getty Images, p. 6; © Sultana/Splash News/CORBIS, p. 7; Gregory Pace/BEImages, p. 8 (right); © Anthony Cutajar/Retna Ltd./CORBIS, p. 9; © Ian MacNicol/Getty Images, p. 10; © Chris Jackson/Getty Images, p. 11; © David Livingston/Getty Images, p. 13; © Brian Lowe/ZUMA Press, p. 14 (top); Robert Keshishian/London Entertainment/Splash News/Newscom, p. 14 (bottom); © Robb D. Cohen/Retna Ltd./CORBIS, p. 15; © Noel Vasquez/WireImage/Getty Images, p. 16; Jen Lowery/Splash News/Newscom, p. 17; © Joey Foley/Getty Images, p. 18; © George Pimentel/WireImage/Getty Images, p. 19; © Brent Perniac/AdMedia/ImageCollect, p. 20 (bottom right); David Tonnessen/PacificCoastNews/Newscom, p. 21; AP Photo/Arthur Mola, p. 22 (top); © AdMedia/ImageCollect, p. 22 (bottom); © Sonia Moskowitz/Globe Photos/ImageCollect, p. 23; © Tupungato/Dreamstime.com, p. 24; © Graham Denholm/Getty Images, p. 25; © Christie Goodwin/Redferns/Getty Images, p. 26; © Michael Kovac/WireImage/Getty Images, p. 28 (top left); © Jeffrey Mayer/WireImage/Getty Images, p. 28 (right); © Chris McKay/WireImage/Getty Images, p. 28 (bottom left); MediaPunch Inc/Rex USA, p. 29 (top left); © Ross Gilmore/Redferns/Getty Images, p. 29 (right); © George Pimentel/WireImage/Getty Images, p. 29 (bottom left).

Front cover: © Byron Purvis/AdMedia/ImageCollect (left); © Slaven Vlasic/Getty Images (right).
Back cover: © Michael Kovac/WireImage/Getty Images.

Main body text set in Shannon Std Book 12/18.
Typeface provided by Monotype Typography.